This book belongs to

a Paul Doodles original

time to get a new notebook

www.ingramcontent.com/pod-product-compliance
Lightning Source LLC
Chambersburg PA
CBHW081602220526
45468CB00010B/2740
* 9 7 8 1 7 9 8 7 1 0 3 5 7 *